A Cat's Life

First published by Parragon in 2010
Parragon
Queen Street House
4 Queen Street
Bath BA1 1HE, UK

ISBN: 978-1-4075-4998-9

Printed in China

A Cat's Life

inspiration for cat lovers everywhere

Bath · New York · Singapore · Hong Kong · Cologne · Delhi · Melbourne

I purr,
therefore I am.

Unknown

There are two means of refuge from the miseries of life: music and cats.

Albert Schweitzer, French-German philosopher and musician

So much
time,
so little to do...

Garfield, Garfield –The Movie (2004)

A meow massages the heart.

Stuart McMillian, Cricketer

Kittens are angels with whiskers.

Unknown

Dogs believe they

are human.

Cats believe they

are God.

Unknown

What
greater
gift
than the love
of a cat?

Charles Dickens, Novelist

A cats **worst** enemy is a closed door.

Unknown

If only cats grew

into kittens.

Robert A.M. Stern, Architect and Dean of the Yale University School of Architecture

The problem
with cats is that
they get the same
exact look
whether they see
a moth or an
axe murderer.

Paula Poundstone, Comedian

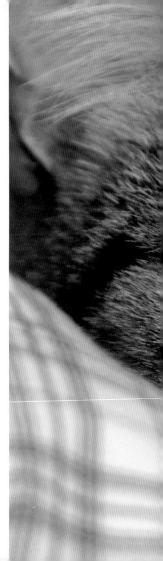

I believe cats to be

spirits come to earth.

A cat, I am sure, could

walk on a cloud

without coming through.

Jules Verne, French author

The dog for the man, the cat for the woman.

Proverb

The smallest feline is a masterpiece.

Leonardo da Vinci, Italian Renaissance artist and inventor

In a cat's world, all things belong to cats.

Proverb

Cats only pretend to be domesticated if they think there's a bowl of milk in it for them.

Robin Williams, Actor

Cats always seem

so very wise,

when staring with their

half-closed eyes.

Can they be thinking,

"I'll be nice, and

maybe she will

feed me twice?"

Bette Midler, Singer and actress

Isn't there always a cat **napping** on whatever you're reading?

Unknown

There is no more *intrepid* **explorer** than a kitten.

Jules Champfleury, French novelist and art critic

Thousands of years ago,

cats were **worshipped**

as gods.

Cats have **never**

forgotten this.

Unknown

The **trouble** with cats is that they've got no tact.

P. G. Wodehouse, Writer

Her function
is to sit and be
admired.

Unknown

A cat has absolute emotional honesty.

Ernest Hemingway, Writer

No matter
how much
cats fight,

there always seems to be

plenty of kittens.

Abraham Lincoln, Former President of the United States 1861-1865

Cats are connoisseurs of comfort.

James Herriot, veterinary surgeon and writer

To err
is human,
to purr
is feline.

Robert Byrne, Writer

Even the **stupidest** cat seems to know more than any dog.

Eleanor Clark, Writer

55

One cat just leads to another.

Ernest Hemingway, Writer

Pussy cat, pussy cat
Where have u been?
I've been to London
To look at the Queen

Pussy cat, pussy cat
What did you there?
I frightened a little Mouse
Under her chair.

Mother Goose

After scolding one's cat one looks into it's face and is seized by the ugly suspicion that it understood every word.
And has filed it for reference.

Charlotte Gray, Canadian Author

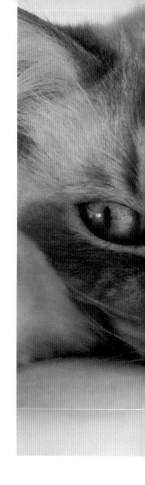

People that don't

like cats haven't met the right one yet. Unknown

Anything not nailed down is a cat toy.

Unknown

It is
impossible
to keep a
straight face
in the presence of
one or more
kittens.

Unknown

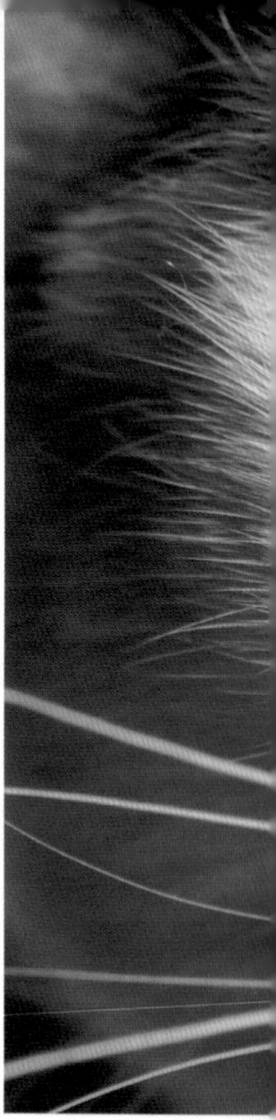

Two things are aesthetically

perfect in the world -

the clock and the cat.

Emile Auguste Chartier, French philosopher

The
ideal
of calm
exists in a
sitting cat.

Jules Renard, French author

Cats are rather

delicate

creatures and they
are subject to a good
many **ailments**,

but I never heard of one who

suffered from insomnia.

Joseph Wood Krutch, Writer and critic

For me, one of the pleasures of cats' company is their devotion to bodily comfort.

Compton Mackenzie, Novelist

Cats can **work out** mathematically the exact place to sit that will cause most **inconvenience.**

Pam Brown, Australian poet

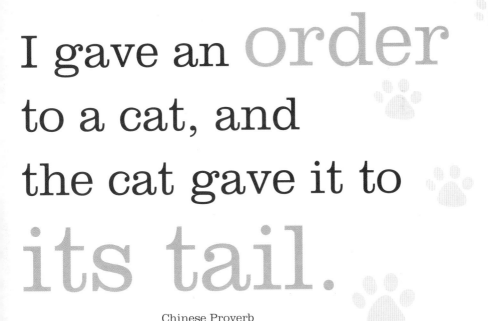

I gave an order to a cat, and the cat gave it to its tail.

Chinese Proverb

Time spent with cats is never wasted.

Colette, French novelist

Some people say man is the **most dangerous** animal on the planet. Obviously those people have never met an angry cat.

Unknown

It's really the

cat's
house

we just pay the

mortgage.

Unknown

I have **studied** many philosophers and many cats.

The wisdom of cats is infinitely superior.

Hippolyte Taine,
French critic and historian

A little **drowsing** cat is an image of a perfect **beatitude.**

Jules Champfleury, French novelist and art critic

He lives in the halflights in secret places, free and alone, this mysterious little great being whom his mistress calls, My cat...

Margaret Benson, Author

The cat
is above
all things,
a
dramatist.

Margaret Benson, author

A cat's a cat and that's that.

American saying

Picture credits